FUN FIGURES

Written, designed and illustrated by
Michael Grater

Macdonald

Fold and stand

Fun figures are easy to make and can be anything you want them to be! All you need are a few simple tools and some old packaging materials that are thrown away every day, such as card, plastic, string, and so on.

Find a piece of card – you could cut it from an opened-out cereal packet – and fold it in half. To make a neat, straight fold you should score along the dotted line with the point of your scissors against a ruler. The fold will help the card stand up. Cut the card to the size of the rectangle shown.

Cut off the curved top corners to make the head and shoulders.

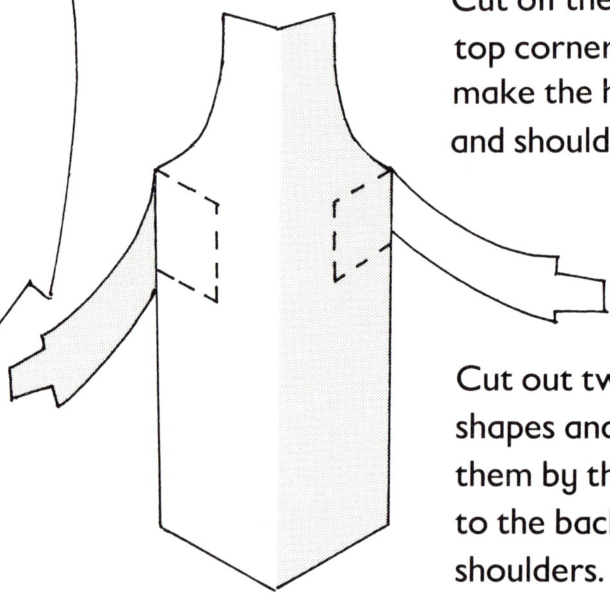

Cut out two arm shapes and stick them by their flaps to the back of the shoulders.

Now you can stand up your first fun figure and think about how you would like to dress it.

You can base your figure on a picture of an historical person, such as Queen Elizabeth I of England. Clothes cut from paper or cloth can be stuck on with PVA glue. Don't make legs too thin or they will not hold up the figure.

You figure's face can be as simple as you like. You can easily draw in some felt-tip features and use frayed string or wool for hair.

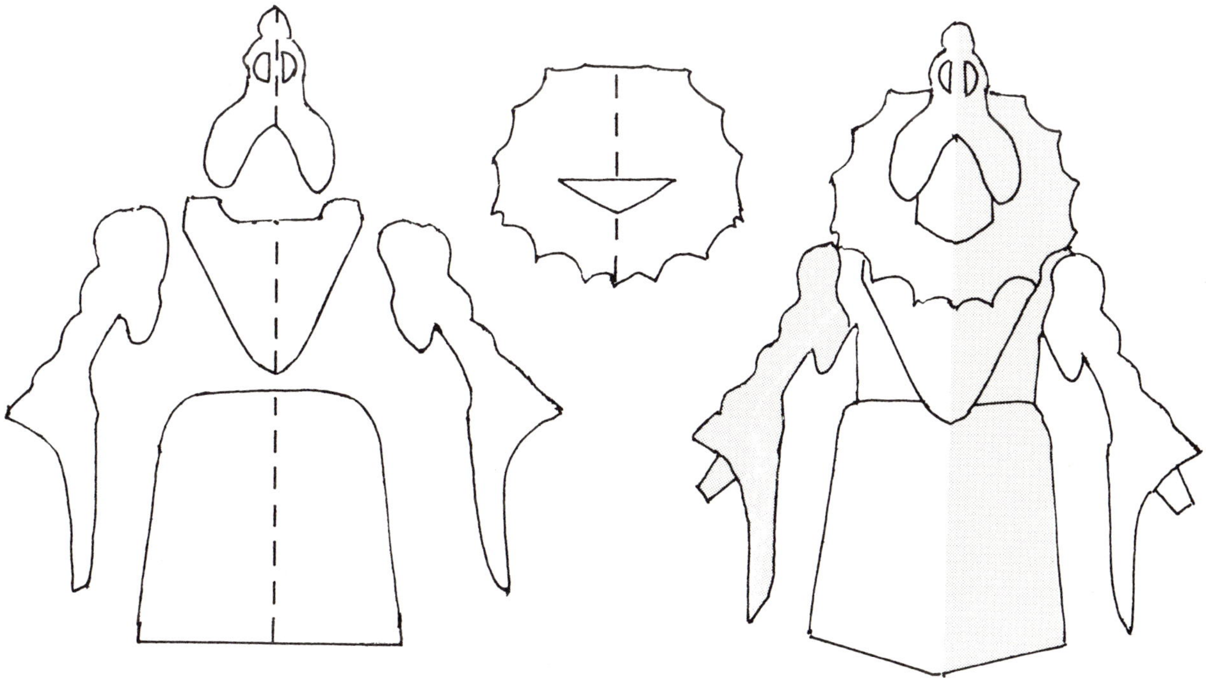

Your figures can be as big as you like, providing the card is strong and stiff enough to stand up when you fold and dress the model.

Rider FUN FIGURES

You can easily make figures on horseback with some card from a cereal pack.

Cut the rider from card folded double down the middle.

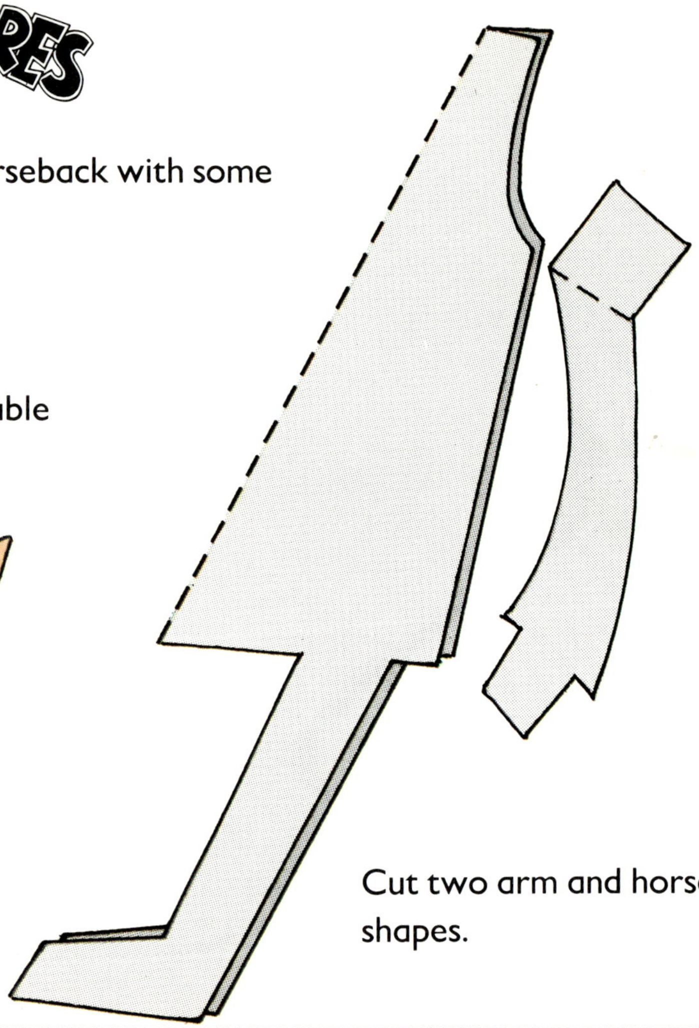

Cut two arm and horse shapes.

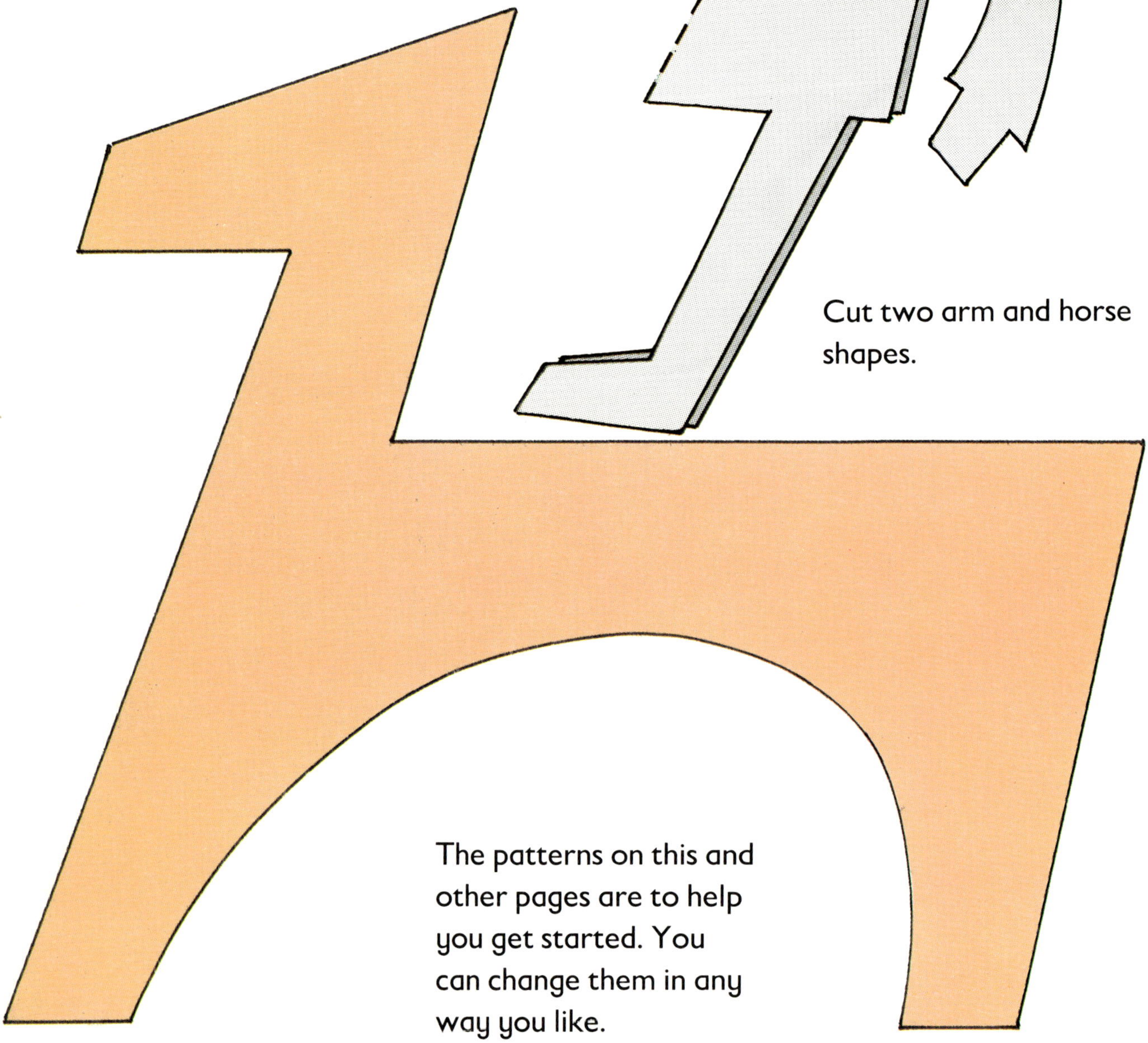

The patterns on this and other pages are to help you get started. You can change them in any way you like.

Fix the arms by flaps to the back of the rider's shoulders. Fray out some string and glue it between the shapes for a mane and tail. Glue or staple the horse shapes together at the top of the head and body.

You may need to strengthen the legs by scoring and gently folding them along the dotted lines.

You can dress the horses and riders in any way you like. Library books will help you with pictures of costume and decoration.

Seated FUN FIGURES

If you cut a standing figure a little shorter in the body you can add legs and turn it into a seated figure.

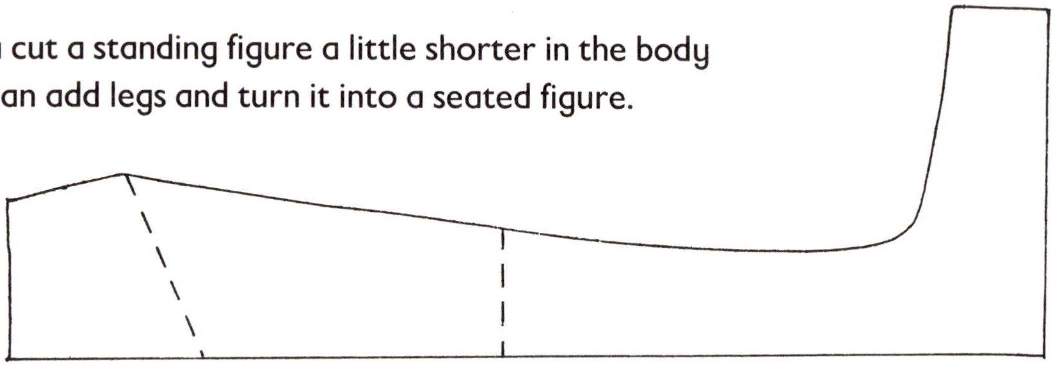

You can make a chair or throne for a seated figure from a box and some bits of card.

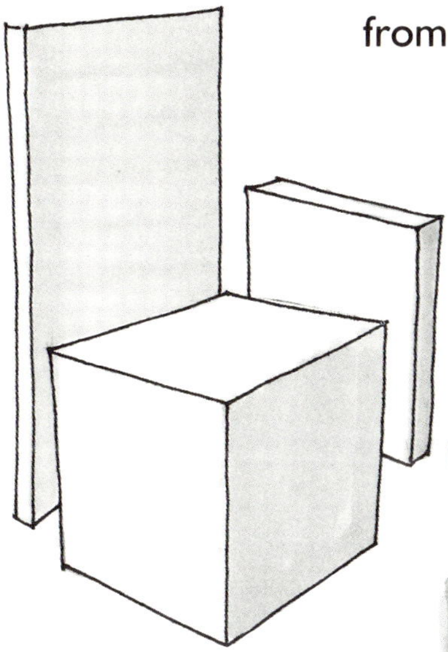

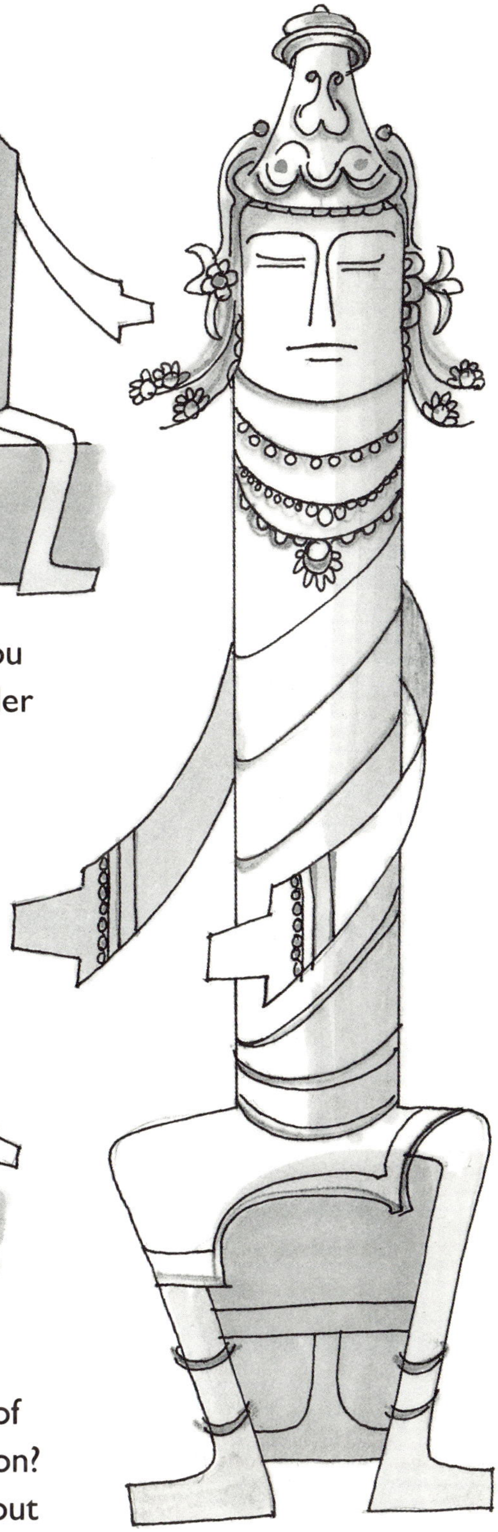

Seated figures can be made with folded card or you can use other salvaged packaging. The card cylinder from a kitchen or toilet roll will sit nicely. Tape or glue some arms and legs and a head to the body.

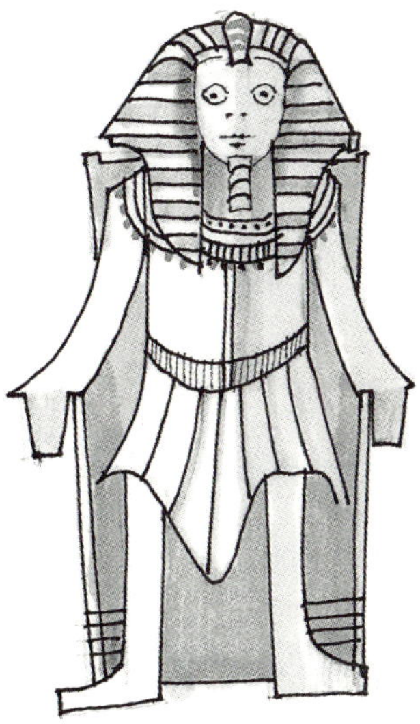

How many different seated figures can you think of from history, stories or from your own imagination? Why not make some figures and write a story about them?

Newspaper FUN FIGURES

You can make all sorts of fun figures with newspaper, string, and adhesive tape.

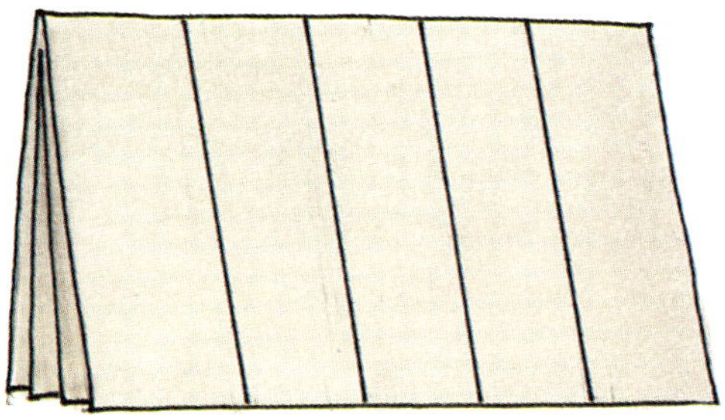

Start with two double sheets of newspaper laid out flat. Measure and cut strips 6.5 cm wide. Cut three pieces of string 75 cm long.

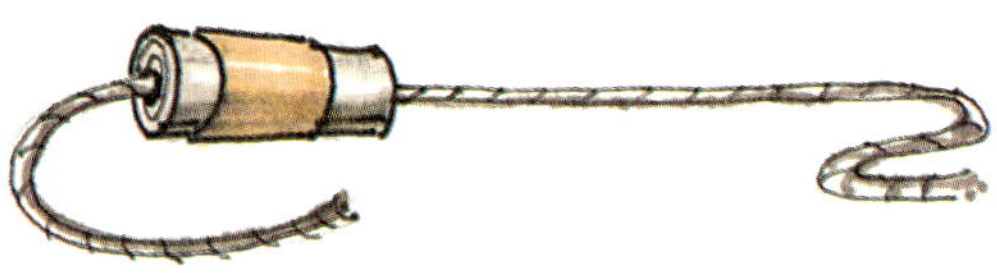

Roll the first paper strip round one of the strings and secure with tape.

Tie off one end of the string so that the roll cannot slip off.

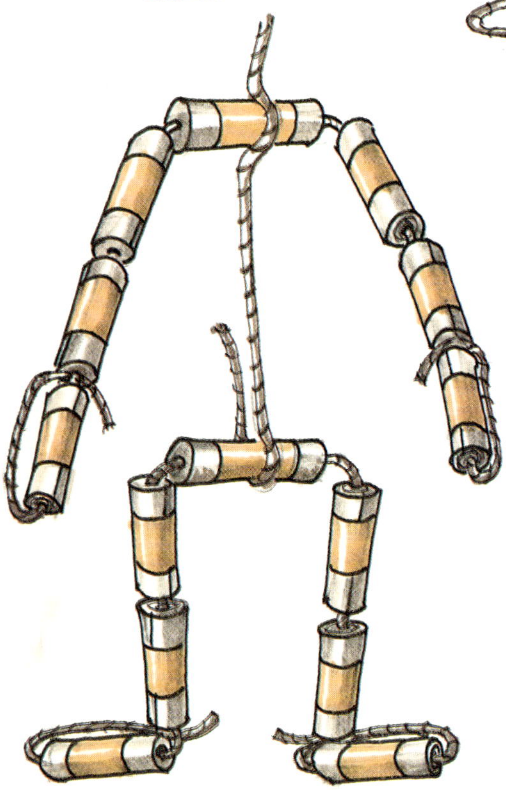

Assemble seven rolls of paper on one string and tie again at the other end. Try not to leave too much space between the rolls.

Make another assembly of seven rolls and fix the end rolls as shown to make feet.

Tie the third string tightly round the middle roll of the legs. Put two more, thicker, rolls on the string to make the body. Tightly loop the string round the shoulders and add another thick roll for a head. Loop the string over and fix it to keep the head on.

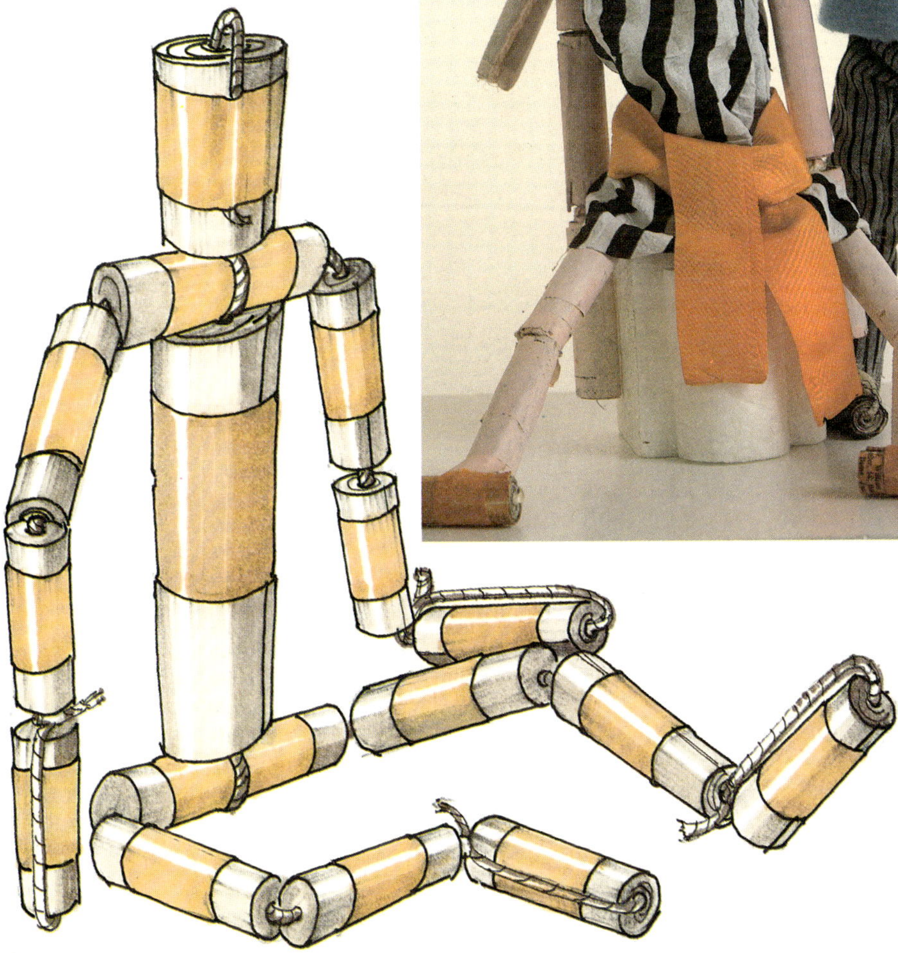

Marionette

Draw a face on your newspaper figure with felt-tips. Even better, model features in plasticine and paste them on with glue and strips of paper.

If you can sew a simple cloth tunic for your figure you can easily turn it into a marionette. Tie a piece of string to a stick you can hold, and tie the other end to the top of the marionette's head. Work the arms with a string loop tied to each wrist. Move the legs with strings tied from the knees to the ends of the wood. If this figure is too loose and floppy, try making it stiffer with sticky tape on the joints.

Try using wire instead of string. By pulling the wire tight enough you can stand or seat the figures in any position. You need to use a wire you can bend with your fingers and cut with pliers. 18 gauge picture wire from a do-it-yourself store works well.

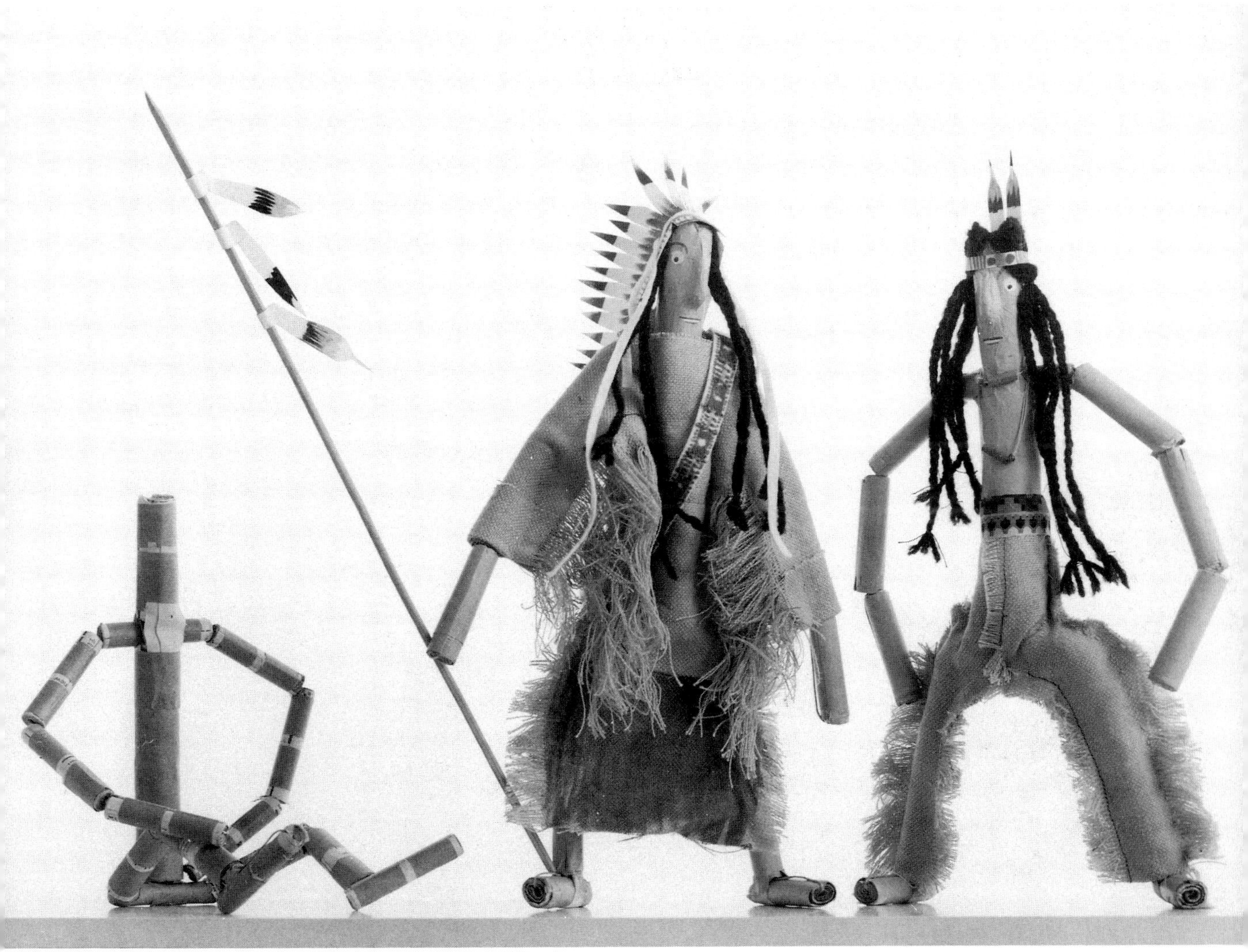

You could use the wire newspaper figures for topics at school. Why not write a play for your marionette figures and produce your own puppet show?

Flat flexible FUN FIGURES

If you have plenty of salvaged card and can work out a way of joining shapes together, you can make all sorts of flexible or moving figures.

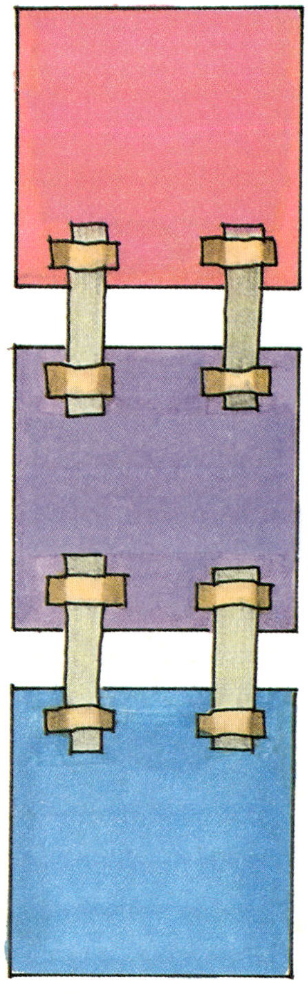

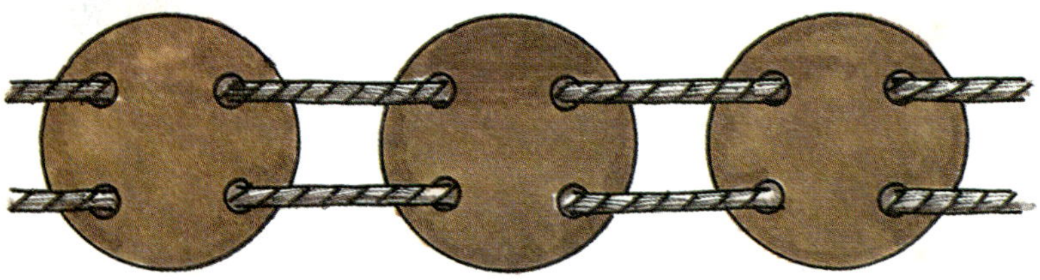

If you use tape you may have to reinforce the sticking point with more sticky tape. If you do, try to do it neatly. All the things you can make in this series of books will turn out better if you take as much care as possible when you make them.

Try measuring and making patterns to decorate your flexibles. With a ruler, compasses, and felt-tips you can discover a lot about shape and colour.

There are lots of shapes you can use but the simplest ones work best, especially if you think carefully about the colours you use.

What can you find out about squares and rectangles?

. . . or triangles?

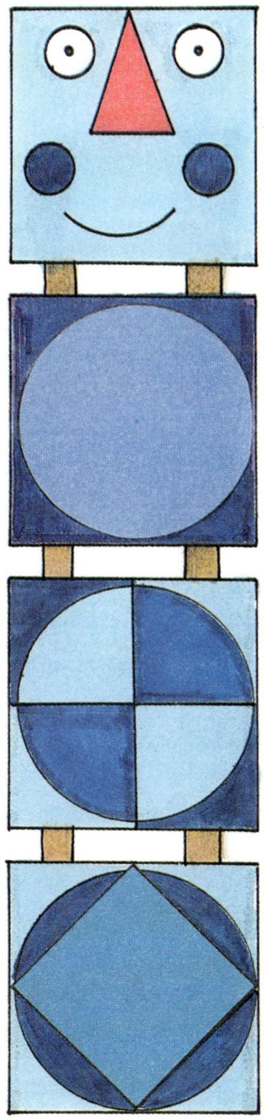

. . . or circles?

How many circles, squares and triangles can you find in these shapes?

Reeler FUN FIGURES

Never throw a cotton reel or spool away, make a collection of them. With some thick string or cord you can make all sorts of friendly reelers.

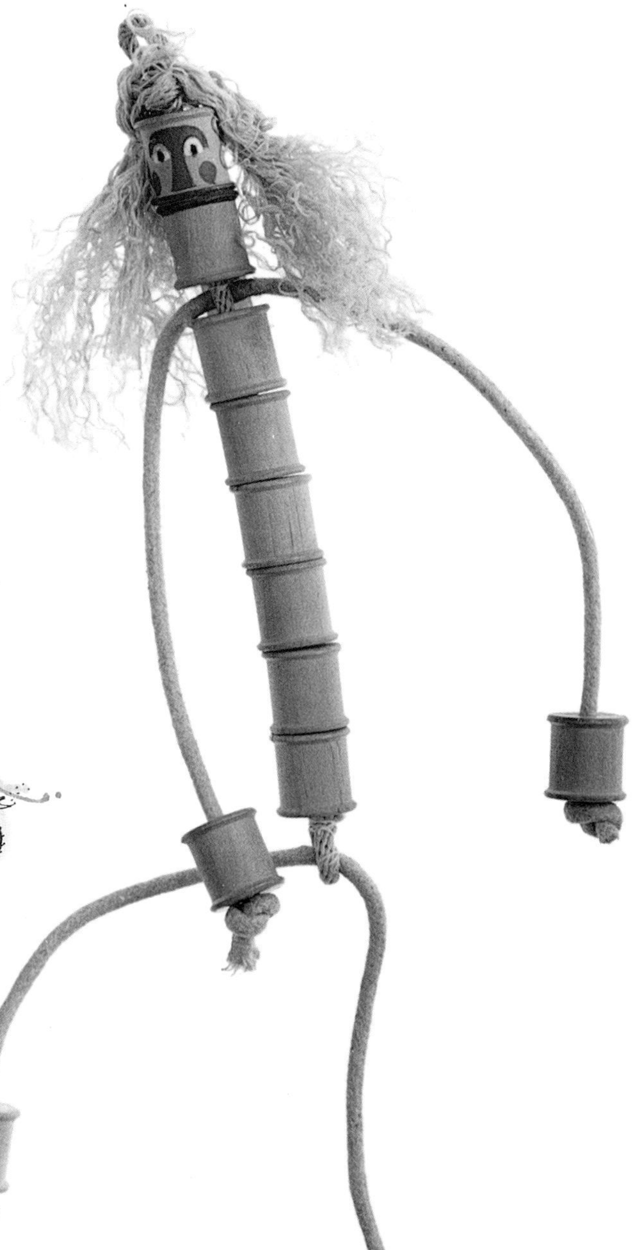

You need two spools for the head, one each for the hands and feet, and as many as you like for the body. Glue on some frayed string or wool for hair.

Lagger FUN FIGURES

You can make laggers, friendly wobbling dolls, with flexible plastic pipe lagging, the sort that is put round copper plumbing tubes.

You can make your laggers very large if you can find some flexible insulated wire. Paint your laggers with paints mixed with a little PVA glue. You can also decorate them with coloured sticky tape. Could you make a reeler or lagger for a friend?

Money box FUN FIGURES

Many sorts of packaging have transparent plastic covers so that you can see what is inside. They make good fun figure money boxes. All you need to do is cut a head and arm shape to match the size of the box – and some simple feet.

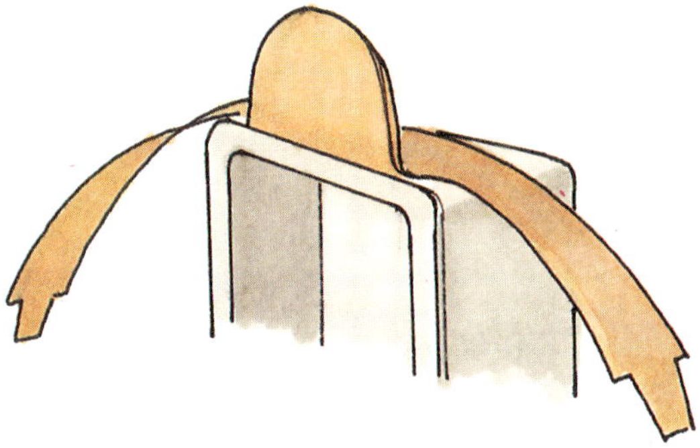

Fold the head and arms and fix them with transparent sticky tape to one end of the box. Carefully cut a slot somewhere at the top of the box so that you can put coins in. Seal the lid neatly to the box with sticky tape. Fix the feet to the other end.

Try making up money box figures of your own. They make very good presents to give to people.

Look out for transparent lids that are specially shaped to fit round things like tools or toys. When these packs are empty they can be turned into all sorts of interesting money boxes.

You can make your money box fun figures stand or sit. You could even hang them up. When your money boxes are full and you are ready to open them, you can easily start again with a different plastic container.

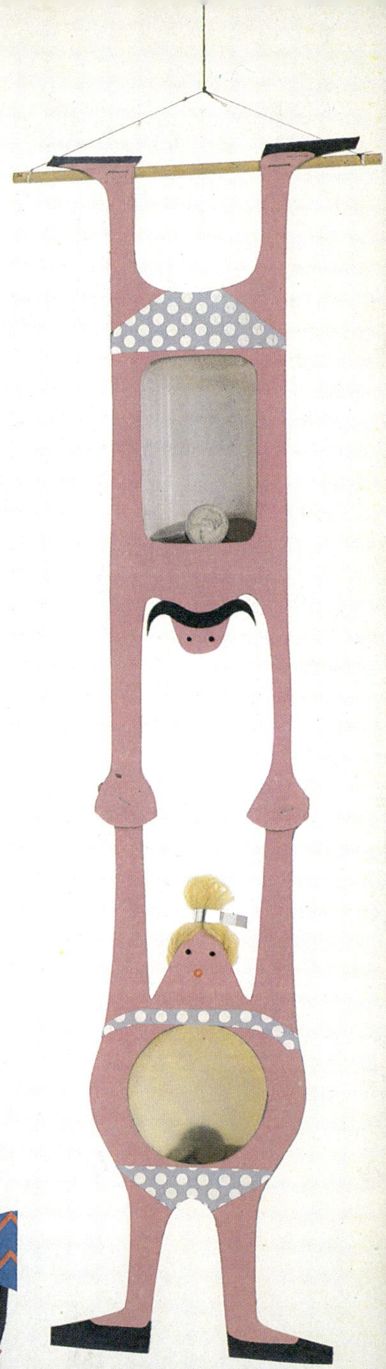

Pocket people

You can make fun figures small enough to fit snugly in your pocket. A wooden clothes peg with a head stuck on can easily be carried with you when you go out.

You can make peg people in team colours, and if you put a happy face at the front and a sad face at the back, you can let the face show whether your team won or lost.

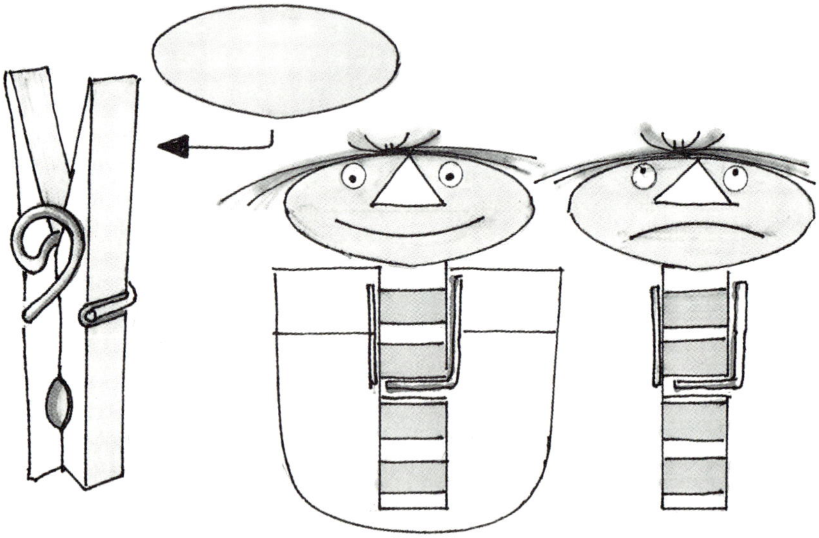

You can make pocket people like Russian dolls which fit inside each other. The patterns opposite are for a family of four. The big doll is shown complete as a two-sided figure with a flap to glue it together. The others must also have two sides and a flap.

Could you make some pocket people to sell to make money for a good cause?

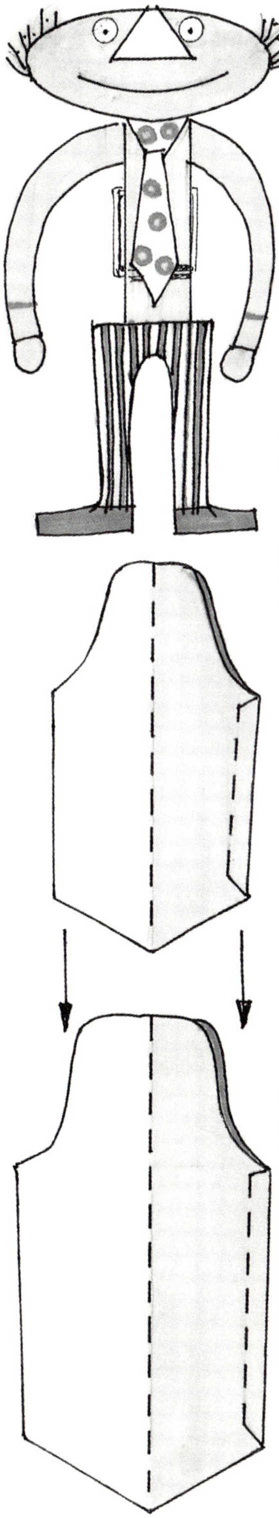

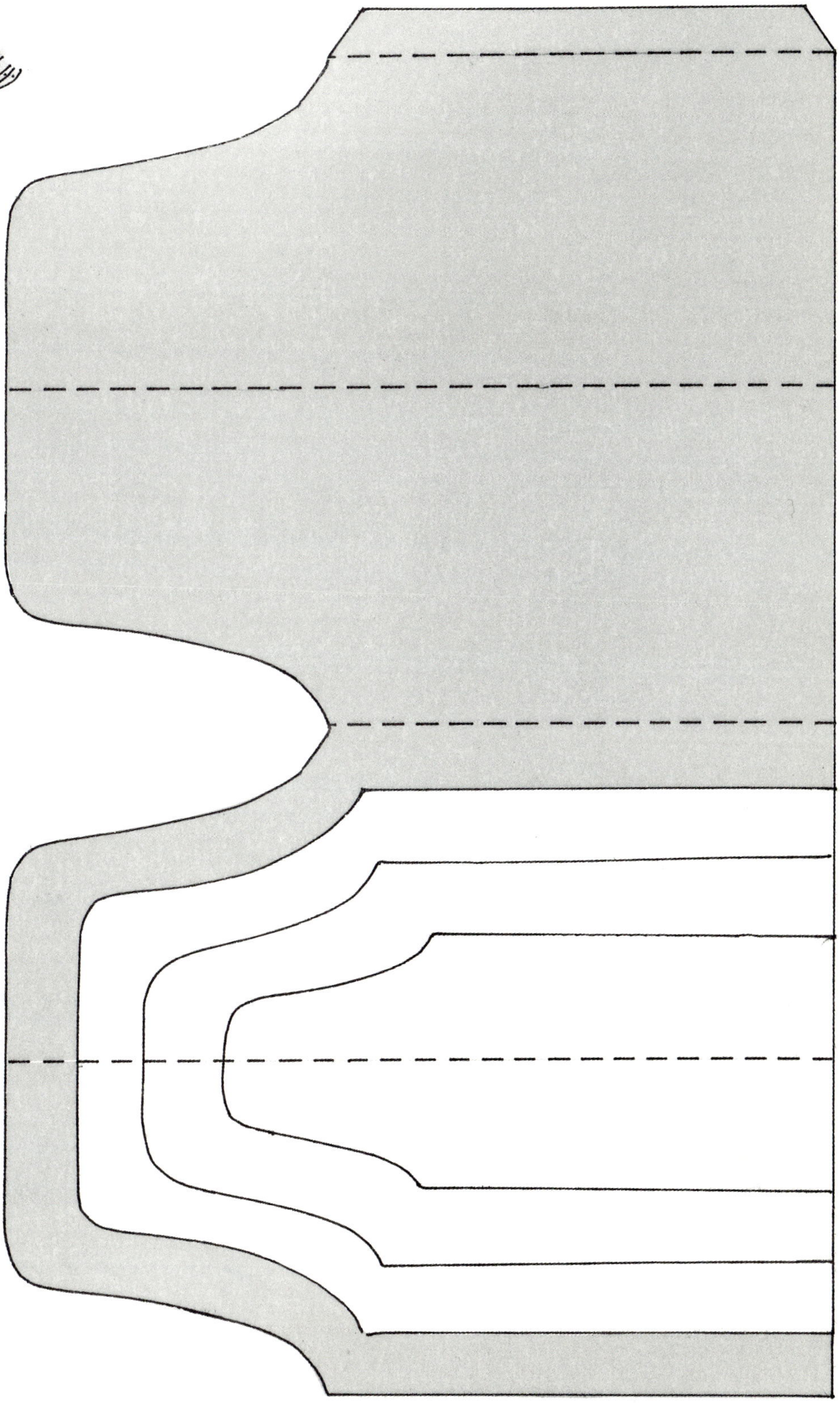

Ventriloquist

If you can find two rectangular plastic packs the same size – margarine packs with flat rims are most suitable – you can put them together to make a mouth which opens and closes.

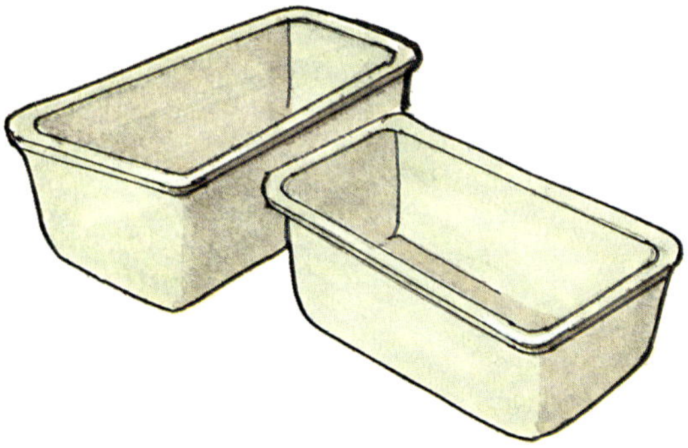

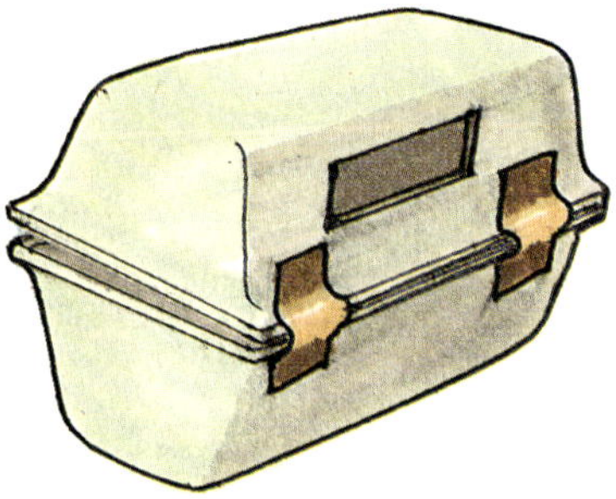

Wash and dry the packs to remove any trace of margarine. Then hinge the packs with sticky tape on one side so that they open and close like a mouth. Cut a hole for your index and middle finger in the hinged side of the top pack. You should now be able to open and close the mouth holding the lower pack with your thumb.

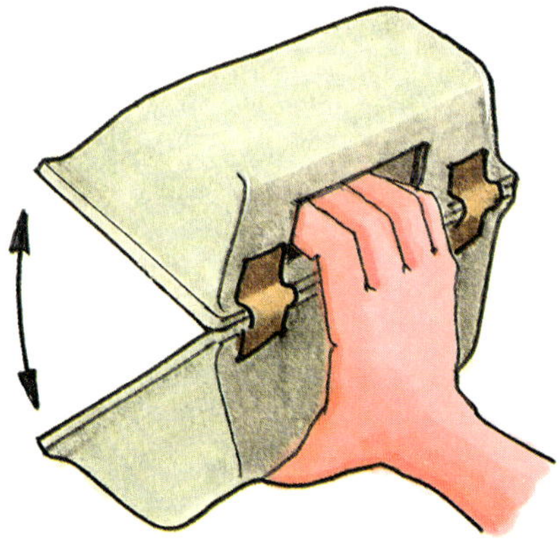

When you can make the mouth move easily you can go on to make a ventriloquist doll. To colour the insides of the packs you must use spirit-based felt-tips, but you will need to experiment to make sure that the ones you have will work on plastic.

Now cut a card shape for the top of the head above the mouth and another for the chin. You can stick these shapes to the fronts of the containers if you use a contact adhesive which works on plastic. When you have a face with a working mouth you can add hair and other features. Now you can learn to be a ventriloquist by talking without opening your mouth!

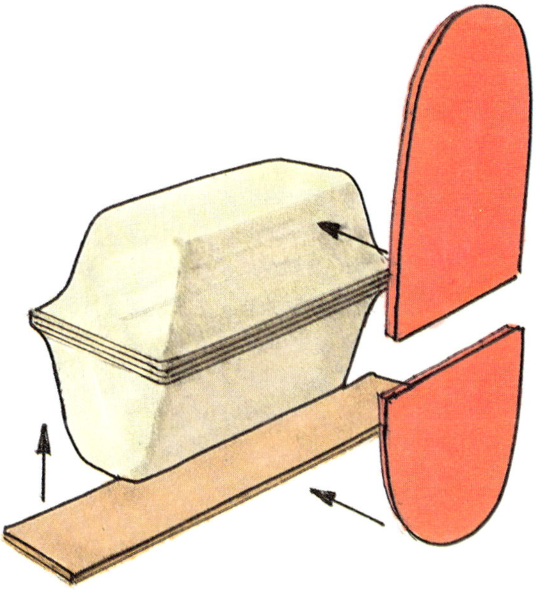

Stretcher FUN FIGURES

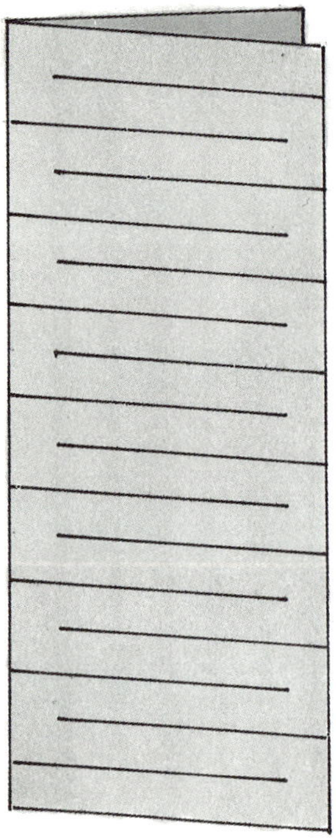

Try making this stretcher from a piece of paper. Fold it in half and draw lines on each side as shown. Use a ruler to get the lines straight and all the same length.

Cut the lines from both sides, making sure you stop exactly where the line stops.

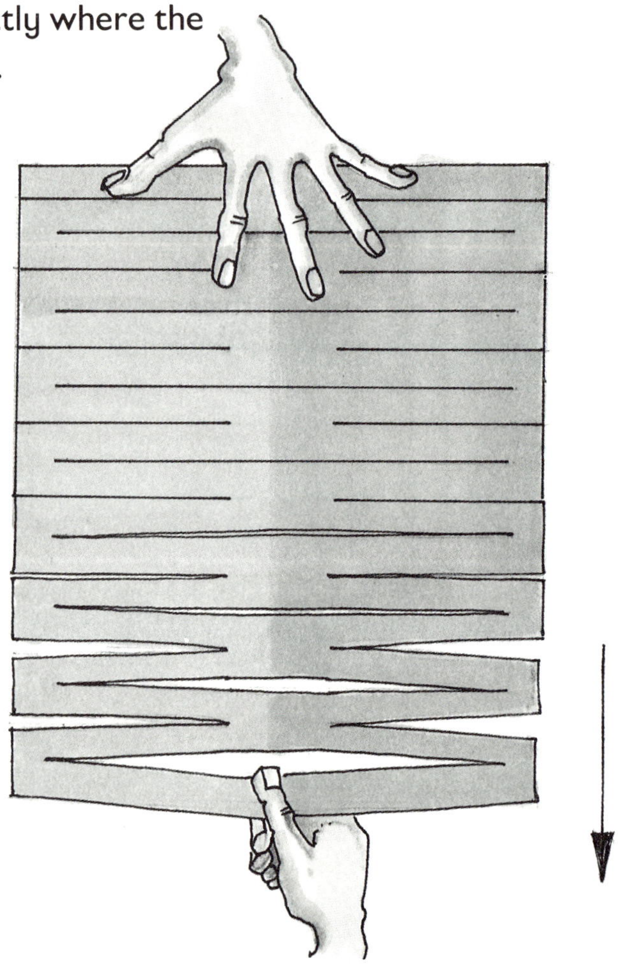

Open the paper out flat. Hold it at the top and pull from the other end.

If you pull carefully, the paper will expand in a neat pattern.

This idea is often used to make paper decorations. You can use it to make stretcher fun figures. Try it on some small sheets of paper to begin with. When you have learned how to cut and stretch the paper, you could make some larger figures.

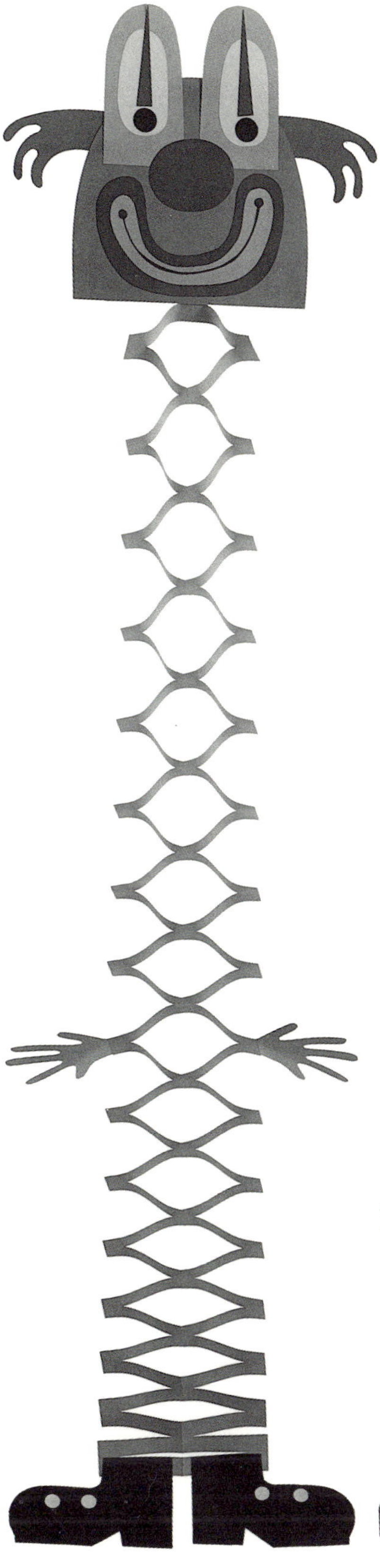

Add a head, some hands, and simple legs and feet to make an unusual fun figure decoration.

You can also make a stretcher from a piece of paper folded twice. Try it and see what happens.

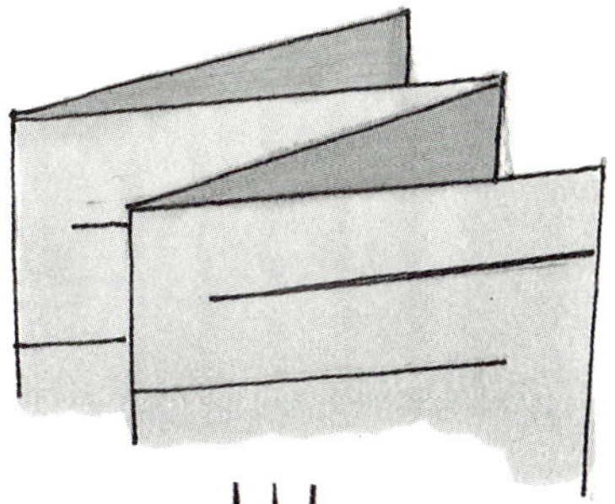

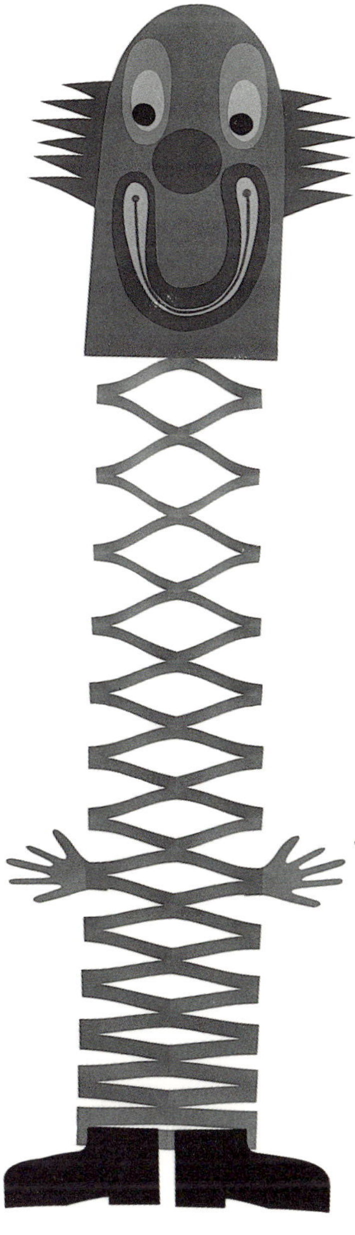

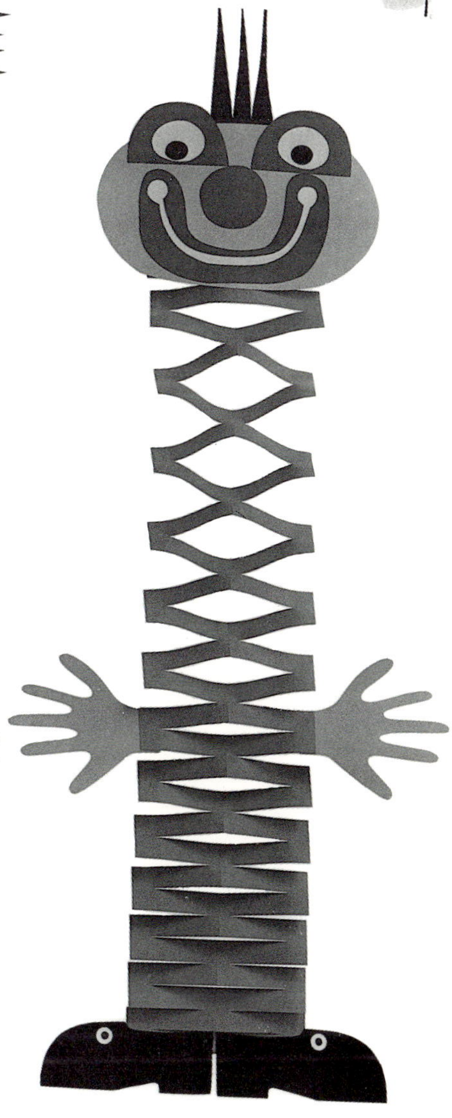

Wobbler FUN FIGURES

Look for the longest strip of stiff paper you can find. It should be about 10 cm wide.

Fold it once . . .

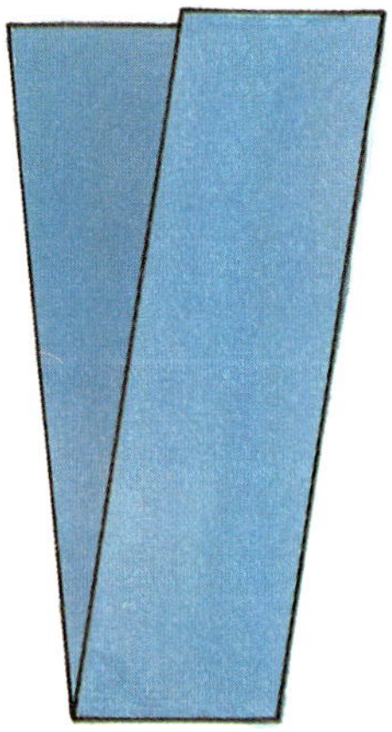

and again . . .

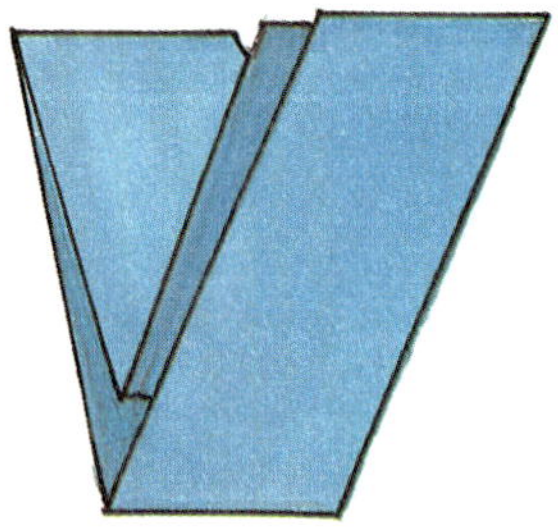

and again.

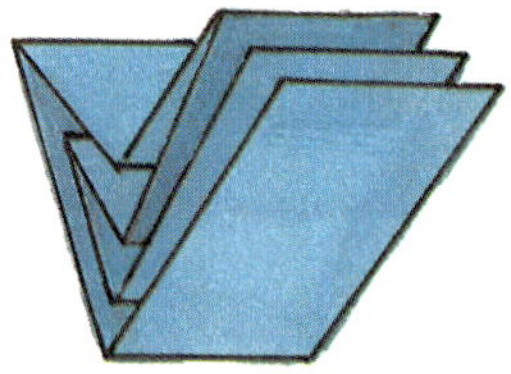

Open it out flat again and refold it as a zig-zag.

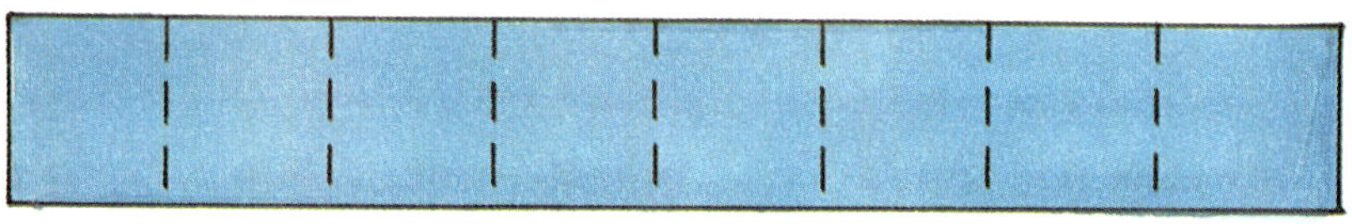

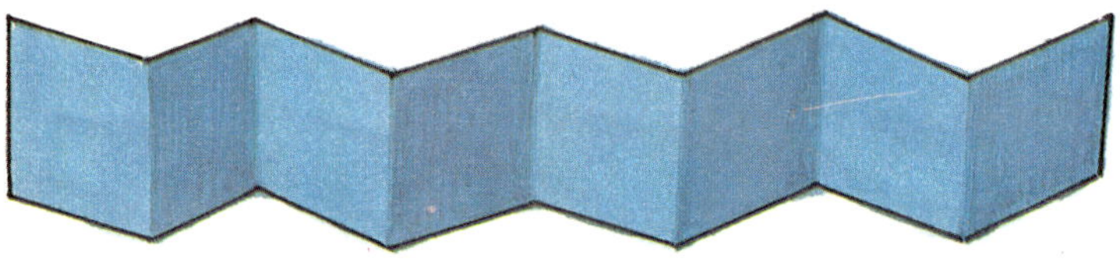

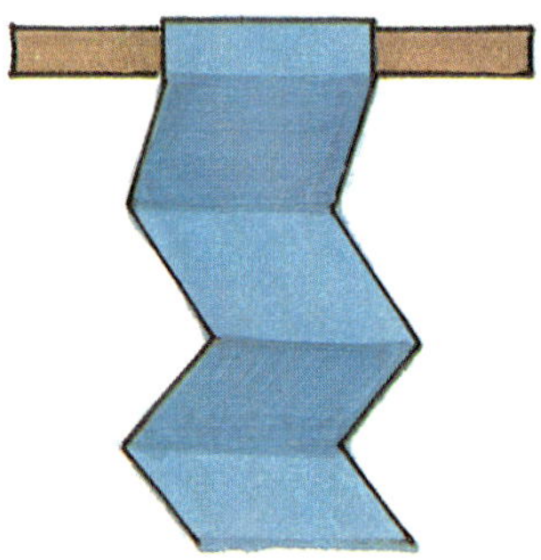

Find a piece of stiff, strong card about 18 cm wide and fix the zig-zag strip in the middle of it.

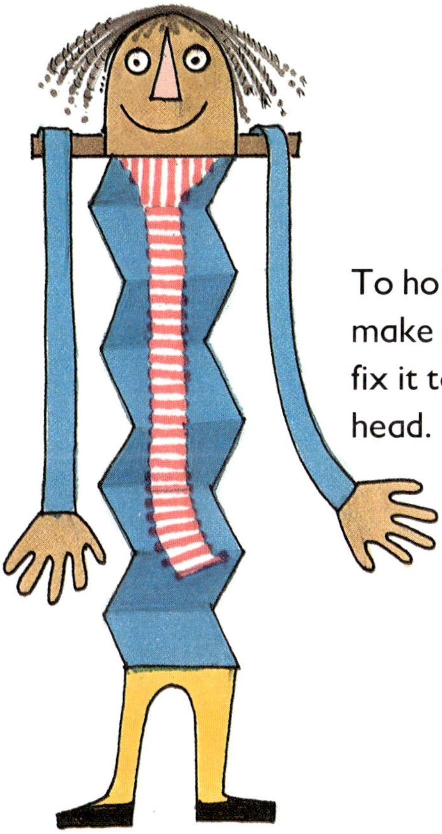

Fix a head and some arms to the card strip, and some legs to the other end of the zig-zag. Now you have a fun figure which you can wobble as you hold it.

To hold the wobbler make a simple loop and fix it to the back of the head.

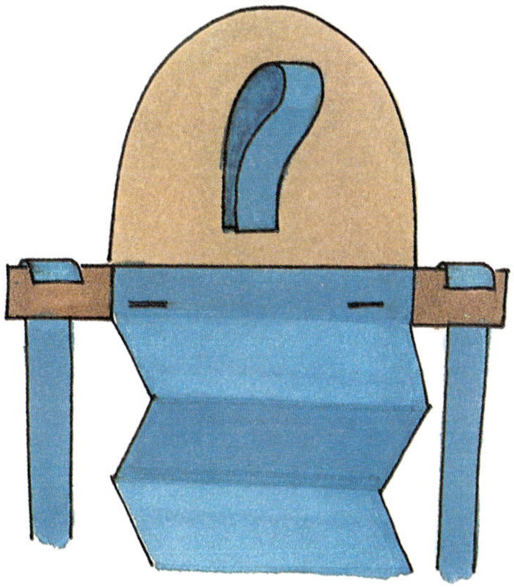

Try making wobblers as tall as you are. You can fix strips of paper together to make longer bodies. You can use the wobblers as decorations but you can also use them as puppets. You could do charades from books you have read or even make up your own characters and stories.

Giant FUN FIGURES

Making a giant is easy. You can make one as large as you have space to hang it. The trick is to have a length of wood for the shoulders, just like the strong card you used for the wobblers.

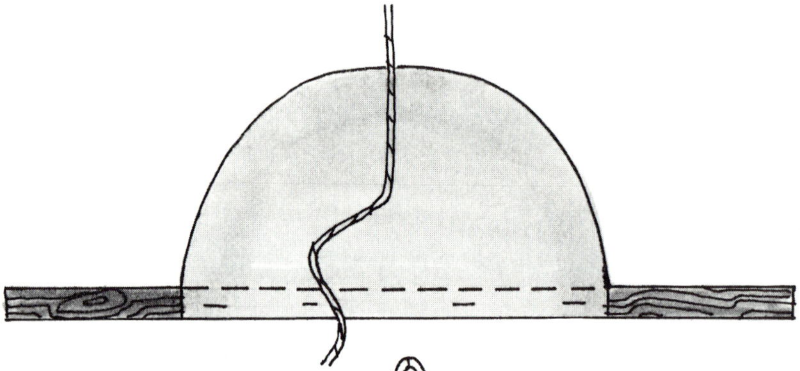

Cut a head from a large piece of stiff card – make sure you give it a strong, thick neck! Fix the head and a long piece of string on to the centre of the wood. When you've added a body, arms and legs you can haul up your giant by the string. You can join together pieces of material with strong sticky tape or staples to make your giant tall enough.

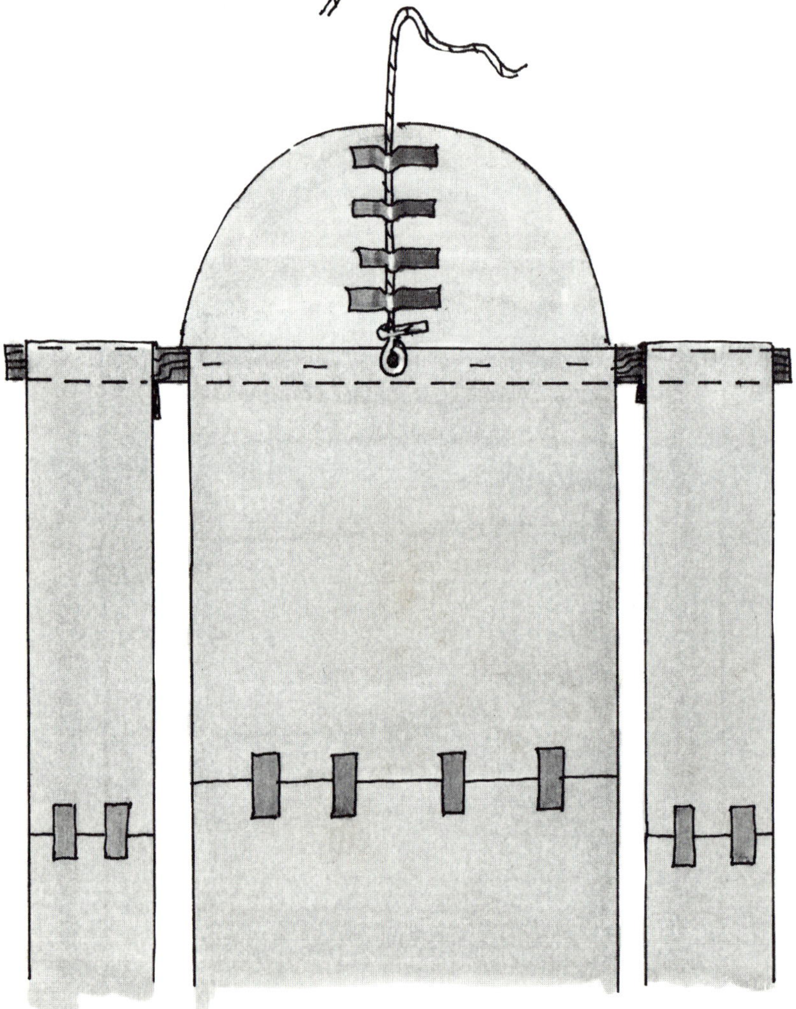

You can use any material for the body and arms – paper, corrugated card, card from cartons, hessian, and so on. Use unravelled bits of wool or string for hair, and bits of scrap cloth to decorate the front of your giant.

Why not fill your school with your own school giants?

Going on with FUN FIGURES

From pocket-people to giants, there are endless fun figures for you to make.

Cut a ghastly ghost shape from newspaper – join sheets together for an extra tall ghost. Fix the top of the head to a strip of stiff card so you can hang up your ghost.

You can make another ghost with thin strips cut from white plastic bags. Cut out a ghostly card head. Tape the head and strips to a strip of stiff card.

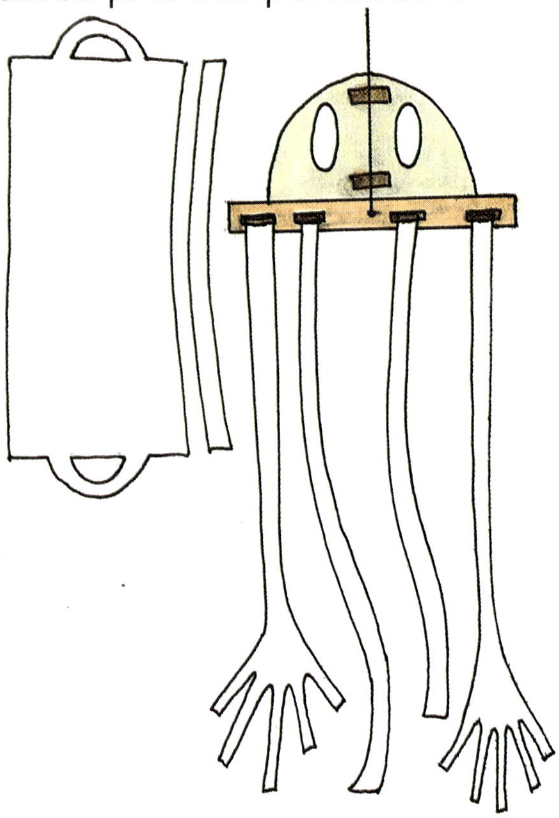

What other fun figures can you think of to make someone laugh? Why not start tonight?